Poetry
and
Devotions
for the
Soul

Sandy Bohon LMHC

ISBN-13: 978-1-7325046-4-6

DEDICATION

This book is dedicated to my good friend,
Rick Petitta,
who inspired me to write poetry.

CONTENTS

CONTENTS

CONTENTS

INTRODUCTION

"'For My thoughts are not your thoughts, neither are your ways My ways,' declares the Lord. 'As the heavens are higher than the earth, so are My ways higher than your ways, and My thoughts than your thoughts.'" (Isaiah 55:8,9)

No human can wholly understand the thoughts of God, but they are revealed through His Word. Through the Bible, we get a glimpse of who God is and how He reveals Himself to mankind. His thoughts become words for us to read and apply to our every need.

Poetry is words used to express feelings and thoughts to help us achieve a better understanding of self and the world around us. This book is written to combine Biblical

passages with poetry so that we can learn more about ourselves and the Lord.

When I was in my thirties, I left my husband and raised three children by myself. These were difficult times, and through my trials, I began writing poetry. With my faith in God and my writings, He saw me through my struggles. If you are going through difficult times, or enjoy reading poetry, I hope that my book blesses you.

The questions are added to help you develop a deeper introspection of God, His Word, and the world around you. They are written to help you formulate ideas you have or have not been thinking about and to deepen your relationship with Jesus.

These devotions may be enjoyed in personal quiet time, or group settings for discussion and interactions.

I pray that my poetry and devotional book brings you closer to the Lord, gives you a better understanding of yourself and the world around you, and blesses your soul.

1. GOD LOVES ALL

The stillness of the pond
　The raging of the sea,
The blooming of a rose –
　And God made me.

The thundering in the storm
　The sky so wide and blue,
The beauty of a butterfly –
　And God made you.

The coldness in the winter
　Leaves changing in the fall,
The sun above so bright –
　And God loves all.

"For you created my inmost being; you knit me together in my mother's womb. I praise you because I am fearfully and wonderfully made; your works are wonderful, I know that full well. My frame was not hidden from you when I was made in the secret place, when I was woven together in the depths of the earth. Your eyes saw my unformed body; all the days ordained for me were written in Your book before one of them came to be." (Psalms 139:13-16)

~ ~ ~ ~ ~

God created mankind different than all his other creatures. He created us from the dust of the earth and breathed into us the breath of life. He designed us with a body, soul, and spirit, and every person is created equal.

The same God also made the heavens and the earth. When we look out over the vast ocean or the immense mountains, we can see God's handiwork. The small ladybugs and the tiny flowers were formed for our eyes to enjoy.

God made each person unique, with different abilities and strengths. God loves us all and wants to have a relationship with each of us.

God created the stillness of the pond and the raging of the seas. God is a diverse God, and He formed us out of the dust of the ground. God created us all different but equal. In what ways are we all equal under God?

"A new commandment I give you: Love one another. As I have loved you, so you must love one another." (John 13:34) How should we apply that Scripture to our lives?

If God created us all equal in His image, how should we treat others?

What are your thoughts about how God knew us before we were born?

Do you think the Lord has a plan for your life? If so, what do you think it is?

The Bible says that God loves us. How can we show our love to Him?

2. THE MOON THAT SHINES

The moon that shines above tonight
　Is shining over you,
And looking up I see its light
　Is shining on me too!

"He who forms the mountains, who creates the wind, and who reveals His thoughts to mankind, who turns dawn to darkness, and treads on the heights of the earth – the Lord God Almighty is His name." (Amos 4:13)

~ ~ ~ ~ ~

Do you ever stop and think that God reveals His thoughts to us? When reading Isaiah, Jeremiah, and other passages in the Old Testament, it says, "and the Lord said," which is His thoughts spoken to us. In the New Testament, Christ is speaking and revealing His thoughts to us. We can see God's design through the universe that He created, and we can get a glimpse of His thoughts through His written Word.

God created the heavens and the earth, and He keeps it running smoothly. The earth keeps turning in space, and the moon keeps reflecting the light of the sun. God created man to have thoughts and emotions. It is in our minds that our thoughts are formed that become actions. In our physical bodies, we can be far from each other, but in our minds, we can be close and stay connected. We have an awesome God.

Where can we get a glimpse of God's thoughts?

What are some of the wonders God created?

The Lord created the heavens and the earth and spoke them into being. He wants to have a relationship with you. How awesome is that!

Reflect on the following:

God created mankind in His image to have thoughts and emotions. We reveal our thoughts to each other by our words.

We can hide our emotions from each other, but they are still there. We can be apart from each other, but they can still be on our minds. Distance cannot keep us apart.

Whether we are in the same room as our loved one, or across the ocean from them, we can still feel their presence. As the moon reflects the light of the sun, so our feelings reflect the thoughts of our soul.

3. THE LORD'S GUIDING'S

Lord, I know you love me
   You take interest in my day,
And when I go adrift
   You gently show me the way.

Of all life's little obstacles
   And all my heartfelt dreams,
You have always been right there
   Walking beside me, it seems.

And looking into the future
   I know You'll guide me along,
You'll surround me in Your love
   And keep me where I belong.

"Your word is a lamp for my feet, a light on my path." (Psalms 119:105)

~ ~ ~ ~ ~

As we travel through this life, we are surrounded by a world that is in darkness. There are obstacles everywhere enticing us to live in the world, and to be partakers of their evil. Numerous are the snares of the wicked. We cannot trust in our knowledge to lead us along and to keep us from stumbling off God's path.

The Word of God is the light that directs us in the darkness. There are too many dangers in life; therefore, we cannot trust our eyesight. We need to depend upon the Word of God as the light that keeps us safe.

The Holy Spirit is the oil that fuels the lamp that keeps our feet on the right path. We don't know where the path will lead us, but we take each step in the light of God's Word. We don't know what the future holds, but we know who holds the future. God is love, and He is taking care of us. With the Word of the Lord being our light, we will avoid the pitfalls of darkness, and rejoice in the light of Jesus.

Think about a time that you were in total darkness and couldn't see anything. Was it scary?

People without God are walking in darkness, spiritual darkness. When a Christian is not walking in God's light, they also do not know where they are going. How are you walking?

What do you think are some of the evils of darkness?

In the verse above, what is the lamp that lights our path?

God wrote the Bible to reveal Himself to mankind, and to give us guidelines for our lives. What are some of the things that the Bible says we should do to be on the right path?

Do you want the Lord's light to guide you on your path in life?

4. CAST YOUR BURDENS UPON GOD

Many times problems arise,
   And, I come to a fork in the road.
My body grows, oh so weary,
   Carrying my heavy load.

And it seems that just this once
   I'll stumble and fall to the side,
As the road grows oh so narrow,
   That once was big and wide.

But at the fork, I hear a voice
   From God away up high,
Cast all your burdens upon Me
   And I will help you by.

And then I think of all the troubles,
   That God has helped me through,
He is willing to guide us along
   If only we'll ask Him to.

"Come to Me, all you who are weary and burdened, and I will give you rest. Take My yoke upon you and learn from Me, for I am gentle and humble in heart, and you will find rest for your souls. For My yoke is easy and My burden is light." (Matthew 11:28-30)

~ ~ ~ ~ ~

When we have problems in our life, we should not be afraid to come to Christ for help. As a child of God, we should seek and search Him out and come with faith that He can help us.

We should not learn how to live our lives through the world system, because that brings disappointments. When we put on Christ's yoke, we are putting on His authority, a yoke of love and guidance through the storms of life. It is a yoke for two, and Christ will share our burdens with us.

The world cannot give us the type of rest that we can receive through following Jesus. The way of the world is chaos and disappointments. Christ has the path of peace and rest for our souls.

We all have problems in life. Some issues we might have had for a long time, others might have recently happened. What do you do with your problems?

What does the world system do for our problems?

The fork in the road represents two paths, should we keep our problems, or give them to God. Which path do you choose?

What does Christ want us to do with our burdens? Who are we to learn from?

Why is Christ's yoke easy, and His burden light?

When we give our burdens to Christ, He gives us rest. What does that mean

5. HOW WONDERFUL AM I

Once was an inchworm
   Crawling along,
Content as could be
   Singing his song.

"All of my friends are,
   So very fast,
But I see all details
   As I inch past."

Then up in the sky
   Flew a large bird,
Soaring and singing
   His song could be heard.

"I'm so high up that,
   Rivers I see,
Mountains and forests
   Pass right under me."

So, if you're an inchworm,
    Or a bird in the sky
God wants everyone to sing
    "How wonderful am I."

"For you created my inmost being; you knit me together in my mother's womb. I praise You because I am fearfully and wonderfully made; Your works are wonderful, I know that full well." (Psalms 139:13,14)

~ ~ ~ ~ ~

God loves us and created us in His image. We should not be prideful and think that we are better than others, nor should we have low self-esteem and think bad about ourselves.

Our self-worth should not depend upon what we do, but who we are in Christ. God has given everyone different gifts and talents so that we may help others and can be used to glorify God. All Christians are in the body of Christ, and we are all brothers and sisters in

Christ. Helping others is one of the ways we find fulfillment in life.

When our relationship with Jesus is right, then we will have a proper perspective of who we are in the world and to God. God wants us to love others, and to Glorify Him.

The Bible says that we are all wonderfully made. Do you agree with that concept?

In what ways are you wonderfully made?

We all have good qualities. List below some of your strengths.

Healthy self-esteem is when we think well of ourselves without being egotistical. How is your self-esteem?

If you have low self-esteem, how can you improve it?

Being content with how God made us is something everyone should strive for. What are your thoughts about who you are?

6. GOD'S LOVE IS ALL ABOUT

Love is not something you can see
　But its effects can be felt,
And when you look around,
　God's love is all about.

"For God so loved the world that He gave His one and only Son, that whoever believes in Him shall not perish but have eternal life. For God did not send His Son into the world to condemn the world, but to save the world through Him." (John 3:16,17)

~ ~ ~ ~ ~

The love of God has existed from eternity. Love is a generic term which includes a love of friendship, brotherly love, parental love, and love of country. God's love for us is different, and 1 John 4:16 tells us that "God is Love." Love is an attribute of God and is a core aspect of His character. God is the perfect example of true love, and He sent Jesus to die on the cross for our sins.

Christ is the Lamb of God who came to earth to sacrifice Himself for our sins. The reason we cannot be good to be saved is that Christ's shed blood is what gives us eternal life. Christ's love for us is what kept Him on the cross to die for the sins of the whole world. Salvation is when we accept the payment that Christ made in our place, and by faith believe that He died for us. Then we can spend eternity with Jesus in heaven.

We cannot see the wind, but we can feel its effects. We cannot see God, but we can know His presence. The verse above is probably the most well-known verse in the Bible. Who does God love?

Who did Christ die on the cross for?

Have you accepted the free gift of salvation through Jesus?

The Bible says that God keeps the world in place. When you look around in nature, can you see the love of God and his handiwork?

Write below some of the ways that you can know God's love.

In what ways has God shown you His love?

7. GOD'S WORLD

God is not in the rain
That hits my windowpane,
Or in the clouds above,
But He sends us His love.

God is not rocks or trees
Small ponds or raging seas,
Nor hills or mountains high
Or rainbows in the sky.

And if you look outside
You'll see the world so wide,
Tigers and birds that sing,
God has made everything.

"You alone are the Lord. You made the heavens, even the highest heavens, and all their starry host, the earth and all that is on it, the seas and all that is in them. You give life to everything, and the multitudes of heaven worship You." (Nehemiah 9:6)

~ ~ ~ ~ ~

One of the characteristics of God is His omnipresence, which, comes from Latin – "Omni," meaning "all." Omnipresence is not pantheism, which means everything is a part of God. Pantheism is sometimes described as God is everything and everyone, and everyone and everything is God.

Another false view of God's presence is deism. This view believes that there is a supreme being or creator who is distinct from his creation and does not play an active role in his creation or the lives of people. Deists believe that God is present but does not interact with mankind.

God, as a spirit, is omnipresent and without beginning or end. He is everywhere, and we can worship Him in any place. The Lord that created the heavens and earth loves us and wants to have fellowship with each of us.

Some false views of God are pantheism and deism. Explain what they teach.

The attribute mentioned above of God is _____. Explain what that means.

What are some of the differences between believing in God, and believing in pantheism or deism?

When I was a small child living in Florida, I would sit outside on the small porch in my little rocking chair, while it rained around me. Do you have pleasant memories of rain falling?

God created nature for our enjoyment. What are some of the different places you have been to enjoy the outdoors?

God is all around us, and so is His nature. What are some things that you see that you enjoy outside where you live?

8. THANK YOU, LORD

Did I thank you Lord today
For the blessings you give me?
   For the birds that sing
   The flowers in spring
And the mountains that I see.

Did I thank you Lord today
For the love, you've shown my way?
   For my partner near
   My children dear
And the love we share each day,

But most of all I thank you, Lord
For Christ that you did give,
   For my sins to pay
   On the cross that day,
And eternal life in heaven to live.

"I will exalt You, my God the King: I will praise Your name forever and ever. Every day I will praise you and extol Your name forever and ever. Great is the Lord and most worthy of praise, His greatness no one can fathom." (Psalms 145:1-3)

~ ~ ~ ~ ~

Sometimes people get so busy in their lives that they don't stop and think about what the Lord has done for them. In other words, we take things for granted.

Most Christians pray every day but do we praise God every day. Do we sit and think about how the Lord created the heavens and earth and keeps everything running smooth? The birds that sing and the flowers that blossom are all reminders of how God takes care of us.

Giving praise to the Lord is a vital part of the Christian's life. It takes our eyes off of ourselves and places it on God. Praising God turns our hearts back to Him and keeps us mindful of all the things He has done for us and how much He loves us. God is worthy of our praise.

How often do the verses above say we should give praise to God?

Why should we give praise to the Lord?

God has done a lot for each of us. Do you think God is worthy of our praise?

The Bible says in 1 Thessalonians 5:17, "Pray continually, give thanks in all circumstances; for this is God's will for you in Christ Jesus." How often should we pray?

Emotionally healthy people think of the positive in their life and do not dwell on the negative. On a scale of 1 to 10, where 10 is positive, and 1 is negative, where do you see yourself on the scale, overall?

We should praise the Lord for the big and little things in our lives. What are some of the big things, and little things, that you can give praise to God for?

9. LET MY LIGHT SHINE

Lord give me the love to see
That we're all sinners saved by grace,
That someday in heaven we'll be
Where we'll see you face to face.

Lord give me the courage to tell
Others about how You died,
On the cross to save us from hell,
So in heaven, they can abide.

Lord give me the wisdom to live
A holy life for you each day,
So to others, I can give
A light to show them the way.

"You are the light of the world. A town built on a hill cannot be hidden. Neither do people light a lamp and put it under a bowl. Instead they put it on its stand, and it gives light to everyone in the house. In the same way, let your light shine before others, that they may see your good deeds and glorify your Father in heaven." (Matthew 5:14-16)

~ ~ ~ ~ ~

Nobody lights a lamp only to cover it up. God does not want us to be lights of the world and then cover up our lights. Christ is the true light of the world, and as the moon reflects the light of the sun, so our lives should reflect Jesus to others.

The world is dark and evil. Through our helping others may we draw others to Christ. Light must be visible, and by our good Christian deeds let others see Christ through us. We should not let things into our life that will dull our light and cause us to be ineffective. The purpose of shining our lights is not to glorify ourselves, but God. May we bring glory to God by letting our lights shine brightly.

What do the verses above say that Christians are?

The Bible says that we live in a dark and evil world. What are some of the things that we may do to dull our lights?

What happens if we do not let our lights shine?

The Bible says Christ is the light of the world, and we are to live in the light as Christ is in the light. What does that mean?

What are some of the things Christians can do to let their lights shine?

What can you do this week to let your light shine?

10. KEY TO HAPPINESS

I wanted fame and fortune
    Instead, I was cold and poor,
I wanted love and happiness
    To enter into my door.

But the knock that came was Christ
    His entering in I did find,
He's the key to happiness
    And my mind before was blind.

"Here I am! I stand at the door and knock. If anyone hears My voice and opens the door, I will come in and eat with that person, and they with me." (Revelation 3:20)

~ ~ ~ ~ ~

God did not create man as robots to serve Him; we have a free will. It is our choice to trust Christ as our savior by faith. It is also our choice to serve Him. Christ will not break down our door but is patiently waiting.

Christ is knocking at our doors, and we are the one who has to open it for salvation and service. Eating food with someone is an outward sign of brotherly love. Christ will eat with those and have fellowship with those who let Him in.

This verse illustrates the persevering love of God. Jesus did not just die on the cross for our sins, He also wants to have a personal relationship with each of us. When we live our lives according to the will of God, then we can have peace on earth that fulfills our soul.

A lot of people think that having fame and fortune will make them happy. There are many rich and famous unhappy people. Why do you think that is so?

Being poor doesn't make people happy, either. What are some of the problems the poor might have?

What might be some problems people have that do not have Christ in their lives?

Christ knocks at everyone's door. Have you opened the door for Christ into your life?

Why would some people not want to open the door to Christ?

Why is Christ the key to happiness?

11. WALKING IN THE WOODS

I love to walk in the woods
Where the trees are big and tall,
And seeing different colors
As leaves changing in the fall.

Sometimes I come upon a stream
Where I walk along its side,
There is a peace in the air
And I feel it deep inside.

I love to see the butterflies
Or birds chirping as I walk,
I know God made everything
And to Him, I silently talk.

"They speak of the glorious splendor of your majesty – and I will meditate on Your wonderful works. They tell of the power of Your awesome works – and I will proclaim Your great deeds. They celebrate Your abundant goodness and joyfully sing of Your righteousness. The Lord is gracious and compassionate, slow to anger and rich in love." (Psalm 145:5-8)

~ ~ ~ ~ ~

When we hear the word meditation, we often think of the practices of Eastern mysticism, which include Yoga, Buddhism, transcendental meditation, and contemplative prayer. Some of their teachings explain that we need to 'hear God's word,' not through the Bible, but through personal revelation, meditation, and self-awareness, and we can become one with nature.

Christian meditation is different and is based on the Word of God and what it reveals about Him. Meditating on Nature is thinking about how awesome God is to create forests, mountains, and oceans for our enjoyment. When we are in nature and thinking about how God created the heavens and the earth, we are meditating of god's creation and His power and goodness.

The verses above are talking about how people in the past talked about God's glorious splendor and majesty and shared it with others. Today we are still talking about God's greatness. Do you talk about God to others?

The verses are talking about meditating on God's greatness. In what ways do you think God is great?

What are some of God's characteristics that are mentioned in the verses above?

"For since the creation of the world God's invisible qualities – His eternal power and divine nature – have been clearly seen, being understood from what has been made, so that people are without excuse." (Romans 1:20) We can't see God, but, we can see what He created.

Have you ever walked in the woods and meditated on the greatness of God and His creation?

Sometimes people get too busy in their lives to sit back and enjoy the beauty of nature. Will you take the time this week to go outside and meditate on God's beautiful world?

12. OPEN MY EYES

Lord, open my eyes,
Help me to see,
All the blessings,
You have for me.

Lord, open my mind,
Help me to know,
Your faithfulness,
That you bestow.

Lord, open my heart,
Help me to feel,
The love You send, and,
Your presence is real.

"I am the vine; you are the branches. If you remain in Me and I in you, you will bear much fruit: apart from me you can do nothing. If you do not remain (abide) in me, you are like a branch that is thrown away and withers; such branches are picked up, thrown into the fire and burned. If you remain (abide) in Me and My words remain (abide) in you, ask whatever you wish, and it will be done for you." (John 15:5-7)

~ ~ ~ ~ ~

Sometimes we might not feel close to Jesus, and the element that may be missing from our lives is the "abiding" in Christ. This abiding is a close intimate relationship with Him.

When we abide in Christ, we are keeping His commandments. When we obey Him, then we will be firmly planted in Him. If the branch is separated from the vine, it cannot produce any fruit. We bear fruit through our connection with Him. When we submit to God and put Him first in our life, we can abide in Him and we will have peace and joy in our lives. Pray that God opens our eyes, mind, and heart so we can feel His presence.

Some people do not understand that Jesus wants to have a personal relationship with each of us. What are your thoughts?

Are you happy with the relationship you have with Jesus? Would you like to increase your relationship with Him?

The verses above say that we need to abide in Christ. What does that mean?

The poem mentions that God is faithful. How has God been faithful to you?

In what ways has God blessed you?

What are some of the ways God has shown His love to you?

13. MY REDEEMER

My Redeemer came to earth,
   To shed His blood for me,
Though I'm the one who sinned
   On the cross, He died for me.

And Satan could not stop,
   No matter how he tried,
Christ hung upon that cross
   For me that day, He died.

If I lose my life on earth
   My treasures in heaven I place,
My life will not be in vain
   When I see Him face to face.

"For it is by grace you have been saved, through faith, and this is not from yourselves, it is the gift of God, not by works, so that no one can boast." (Ephesians 2:8,9)

~ ~ ~ ~ ~

Some people have been taught that if you are a good person, then you can go to heaven, and if you are a bad person, then you can't go to heaven when you die. That is not what the Bible says. The Bible says that we are all sinners and that we can't get to heaven with sin on us. Being good, reading our Bible, praying, or going to church, do not take our sins away.

Christ came to earth to die on the cross for everyone's sins because we cannot be good to go to heaven. He became sin for us in our place. All we have to do is trust in the payment that Christ made. We have to believe that Jesus died on the cross for our sins in our place and that He is giving us eternal life.

If we could be good and go to heaven by what we do, then Jesus wouldn't have had to die for us. Trusting in Him is what washes our sins away. When we accept His payment by faith, then we have eternal life.

According to Ephesians 2:8,9, is salvation a gift or a reward?

If salvation is a gift, then do we have to give our lives to God to be saved? Do we have to read our Bibles or pray to be saved?

What do you think a person has to do to receive eternal life?

The Bible says that salvation is a gift and is free to us. We can't go to heaven with sin on us. Who died on the cross for our sins?

If Jesus died for our sins, do we have to?

Salvation is free by faith in Christ. If you haven't already trusted Jesus as your Savior, will you trust Him now?

14. BROKEN HEART

Among the remains
  Of my broken heart,
Is the beginning
  Of a new start.

"The Lord is near to all who call on Him, to all who call on Him in truth. He fulfills the desires of those who fear Him; He hears their cry and saves them." (Psalms 145:18,19)

~ ~ ~ ~ ~

In life, circumstances and relationships do not always turn out how we want them to. We end up with broken hearts. Sometimes there are things in us that need to be broken, such as self-will, pride, and sinful habits.

During the Last Supper, Christ took the bread and said that it was His body which was broken for us. His death made it possible for us to become whole.

Amid our brokenness, Christ calls us to come to Him for healing. Sometimes we don't turn to Christ because we are so busy with other things, our problems, and unhappiness.

When we turn to God and cry out to Him, He is there to heal us. When we focus on God and put Him first in our lives, then He can turn our broken heart into something beautiful for Him. He can turn our brokenness into a life that can bring glory to Him.

Have you ever had a broken heart? How did you handle it?

Are there things in your life that should be removed, such as pride or selfishness?

There is a saying that God breaks us to be His. What does that statement mean?

How was Christ broken for us?

What does it mean to come to Christ for healing?

How can we have a new start in life after having a broken heart?

15. TREASURES IN HEAVEN

My body grows old and weary,
My life on this earth is through,
Looking back, I'd change nothing,
For a secret in life, I knew.

Riches and power are fleeting,
At the grave, they are left behind,
If you live your life for Christ,
Then treasures in heaven you'll find.

"Do not store up for yourselves treasures on earth, where moths and vermin destroy, and where thieves break in and steal. But store up for yourselves treasures in heaven, where moths and vermin do not destroy, and where thieves do not break in and steal. For where your treasure is, there your heart will be also." (Matthew 6:19-21)

~ ~ ~ ~ ~

The Bible states that those who do things on earth for the praise of men will receive their reward on earth. Those who do things for Jesus will receive their reward in heaven.

Life on earth is fleeting, and we will be in heaven forever. When we live for things of the earth and put worldly things in our hearts, then our treasures will be on earth, and they will be left behind. While on earth, our life will be chained and enslaved to our treasures here.

When we serve Jesus and put Him first in our lives, then our treasures will be in heaven, and they will be waiting for us. What treasures we have stored in our heart will come out in our actions. Do you have treasures placed in heaven?

The Bible says that when we do things for Jesus, then we will have treasures in heaven. What things have you done for Jesus?

When we win an award, it is not so much the award, but the time and energy that we put into earning that reward. When we see Jesus, it will be the time and energy that we put into our relationship with Him and the things we have done for Him. How is your relationship with Jesus?

What things are you doing now to increase your relationship with Jesus?

"And now, dear children, continue in Him, so that when He appears we may be confident and unashamed before Him at His coming." (1 John 2:28) This verse is talking about how some people will be ashamed when Christ comes. Why do you think they will be embarrassed?

The poem is looking back at a life who had lived to serve God, and they will be happy to see Him. Will you be ashamed, or will you be rejoicing to see the Lord?

Looking forward, what things can you do, or are doing, to have treasures in heaven?

16. WHY

Why was I born on this earth
What purpose is there for me,
I feel my wheels keep spinning
Like waves on an endless sea.

Even though I'm a Christian
I feel life passing me by,
And so, I will turn to God
And silently ask Him why.

I know He has the answer,
Reading God's Word, I did find,
"Trust in me, and you will know
One day on the other side."

"...or because of these surpassingly great revelations. Therefore, in order to keep me from becoming conceited, I was given a thorn in my flesh, a messenger of Satan, to torment me. Three times I pleaded with the Lord to take it away from me. But He said to me, 'My grace is sufficient for you, for My power is made perfect in weakness.' Therefore I will boast all the more gladly about my weaknesses, so that Christ's power may rest on me. That is why, for Christ's sake, I delight in weaknesses, in insults, in hardships, in persecutions, in difficulties. For when I am weak, then I am strong." (2 Corinthians 12:7-10)

~ ~ ~ ~ ~

We all go through trials and tribulations in life, and things may happen to us, and we don't know why. Paul had seen visions which could have made him conceited and proudful, but God had kept him humble by allowing him to have a thorn in his flesh.

Sometimes we go through things that seem unbearable, and we don't understand why. What we are struggling through might be a spiritual, emotional, or physical problem, but God has a purpose, and His grace is all-sufficient. The Lord is faithful and will take care of us.

Paul had a thorn in his flesh, but the Bible never said what it was. Do you believe that you have a thorn in the flesh?

What do you think it is, and how long have you had it."

Sometimes when we have trials, we understand why we went through them. Other times we don't. Will you be satisfied never to know, and trust God to see you through?

Do you feel like a hamster on a wheel that is going around and around? Do you feel like life is passing you by?

Do you believe that God has a purpose for your life?

Do you feel that God's grace is sufficient for each of us?

17. GOD'S WILL NOW

I feel I want to move on
But I don't know where to go,
I wish God would speak to me
His will for me He'd show.

But God did speak to me,
"You're in My will now," said He.

"And when the time is ready
The doors will open wide,
Everything will be prepared
All you'll do is step inside."

"But godliness with contentment is great gain. For we brought nothing into the world, and we can take nothing out of it. But if we have food and clothing, we will be content with that." (1 Timothy 6:6-8)

~ ~ ~ ~ ~

Sometimes we may feel discontent in our lives and wish we were further along than we are. We want to be the head pastor instead of associate pastor, or on the mission field instead of being a Sunday school teacher. Maybe we are in the circumstances in life that we wish we weren't in, or maybe feel like we are stagnating and want to be in the future.

God wants us to be content with what we have now. Living in the future cause's anxiety and living in the past may cause depression. We need to live in the moment. Life is a journey, and we need to appreciate what God is doing for us now. We ought to enjoy the moment.

When we are not content in the present, then we are saying that God isn't providing for us. No matter what our circumstances, we should be thankful and trust in the Lord's provisions. Be patient and wait on the Lord's leading.

In counseling, when people are anxious, there is a technique that is called the Mindfulness Technique. The person is to be in the moment, observing things around him, concentrating on what he is doing at the moment. This technique is used to reduce anxiety or depressive symptoms and have the person be in present time.

Make a list below of some of the good things in your life, for example; I have a roof over my head. Try to think of at least 10 or more items.

Being content with what we have doesn't mean we don't have long term goals. What are some of the things you would like to accomplish in the future?

Sometimes people forget about the things they have accomplished and downplay their achievements. Write down some of the things that you have done that you are proud of.

In what ways can you live and enjoy the present?

18. SERVING CHRIST

Whatever life may bring my way
   My hopes and dreams
   Or evil things,
I hope that I can always say
   I trusted You
   To see me through.

But if things do not go right,
   To not give in
   And not to sin,
I hope I can stand up and fight
   For victory win
   For I serve Him.

And if things are going well,
   For me to see
   That Christ helps me,
And that I may always tell,
   That God above
   Sends me His love.

"As for everyone who comes to Me and hears My words and puts them into practice, I will show you what they are like. They are like a man building a house, who dug down deep and laid the foundation on rock. When a flood came, the torrent struck that house but could not shake it, because it was well built. But the one who hears My words and does not put them into practice is like a man who built a house on the ground without foundation. The moment the torrent struck that house, it collapsed, and its destruction was complete." (Luke 6:47-49)

~ ~ ~ ~ ~

We are all builders of our moral and spiritual lives. We are planning, laying the foundation, and building the walls. We can spend time developing a great name or fortune, but they are not sufficient for satisfaction in our lives.

When we build a home, it is easier to construct it upon sand than rock. It will take more effort, but we need to build upon the foundation that is Christ. Build on the conviction that we owe everything to God. When our lives are built on the solid Rock, when storms come, we will be secure in Christ.

The verses above talk about two houses being built, one on the sand, and the other on rock. Is it easier to build on sand or rock? Why?

Who does the rock represent?

The verses are talking about our spiritual foundations. Are you building your house on sand or rock?

Everyone has storms and trials in their lives. What are some of the trials you have been through?

Did you trust in Christ to see you through the storms and tribulations?

The verses above are talking about putting God's Word into practice. What are some of the things that you are doing to build upon the foundation of Christ?

19. LOVE IS LIKE THE OCEAN

Love is like the ocean
Its depths cannot be known
But we can see
The gentle waves,
Upon the beach are blown.

"The Lord said, 'Go out and stand on the mountain in the presence of the Lord, for the Lord is about to pass by.' Then a great and powerful wind tore the mountains apart and shattered the rocks before the Lord, but the Lord was not in the wind. After the wind there was an earthquake, but the Lord was not in the earthquake. After the earthquake came a fire, but the Lord was not in the fire. And after the fire came a gentle whisper. When Elijah heard it, he pulled his cloak over his face and went out and stood at the mouth of the cave. Then a voice said to him, 'What are you doing here, Elijah?'" (1 Kings 19:11-13)

~ ~ ~ ~ ~

After Elijah's victory on Mount Carmel where the fire from God burned up the sacrifice, Elijah became anxious and hid from Jezebel because she wanted to kill him. God spoke to Elijah in the verses above. God didn't speak to Elijah in the earthquake or fire but by a gentle whisper.

God is all-powerful, and we cannot see Him in our human body, or we will be consumed.

We cannot see God, but all the power that created the ocean can be seen in the gentle waves. Just as we cannot see love, we can feel its effects.

God's power created the mountains, the earth, and the stars. He showed His strength to Elijah, but He spoke to him in a calm voice. Why do you think God showed his power to Elijah?

The Bible states, "...God is love." (1 John 4:8) Some people have wrong perceptions of God. Do you think God is love?

In what ways can you feel the love of God in your life?

We cannot see love, but when we look into our lover's eyes, we can feel the love they have for us. We can see the love in the smile of a child. In what other ways can you see love from another person?

What are some of the ways can you show love to others?

In what ways can you show love to God?

20. MEMORIES

Life is a maze of unopened doors
That we pass through one by one,
Through some, we stop and ponder
Through others, we want to run.

Each door slowly opens to us
And we quickly chance inside,
Will we enjoy this season?
Do we want to run and hide?

No matter what each door brings
It will soon be left behind,
We pray that God will bless us
And sweet memories we will find.

"Trust in the Lord with all your heart, and lean not on your own understanding; in all your ways submit to Him, and He will make your paths straight." (Proverbs 3:5,6)

~ ~ ~ ~ ~

Life is very unpredictable, and there are numerous temptations around that want to keep us from following the Lord. When you walk in a field or forest and go over and over the same way, you create a path. Life is a journey, and there are many paths we may take. Some lead to joy and happiness, and others point to sorrow and disappointments.

We do not know what is best for our lives, and we don't see the future. That is why we need to trust Jesus to guide and direct us. We need to seek His will in our lives, and not get off on the ways that lead to loneliness, despair, regrets, and heartaches in life. We should put Jesus first and stay on His path, the straight path that leads to knowing Jesus and having fellowship with Him. Only through Jesus can we find pure joy and peace.

What are some of the right paths you have been on in your life, for example, education?

We all do things in the past that we wish we hadn't done. What are some of the wrong paths that you feel that you had been on in your life?

What things do you think led you to get on the right or wrong path?

What path in life do you feel that you are on now? Do you want to be on that path, or want your life to go in another direction?

The verses above say we should trust in Jesus to guide and direct our lives. Christians believe that God opens and shuts doors. What does that mean?

Write down some of the sweet memories you have from your past.

21. CHILDREN OF LIGHT

There is a gulf between darkness and light,
Between Satan and following the Lord,
There is a ship that sets out to sea,
That all Christians should be aboard.

The earth left behind is the darkness,
The ship out to sea is the light,
The earth is the world and its pleasures,
Where Satan, his demons do fight.

We shouldn't live our lives in the world,
For in Christ we are children of light,
By leaving the world in darkness behind,
We live in the ship of God's might.

"For you were once darkness, but now you are light in the Lord. Live as children of light (for the fruit of the light consists in all goodness, righteousness and truth) and find out what pleases the Lord. Have nothing to do with the fruitless deeds of darkness, but rather expose them. It is shameful even to mention what the disobedient do in secret. But everything exposed by the light becomes visible – and everything that is illuminated becomes light. This is why it is said: "Wake up, sleeper, rise from the dead, and Christ will shine on you." (Ephesians 5:8-14)

~ ~ ~ ~ ~

It is not a safe place to be in the darkness. Sin and corruption are expressed as darkness, while holiness and purity as light. As children of light, we are to keep ourselves from participating in evil and darkness.

When we are living in the light, we are in God's safety and are free from fears and dangers. God wants us to walk as children of light, and to keep ourselves unspotted from the world. Then we will know Jesus and have fellowship with Him.

What is the difference between darkness and light?

The verse above states that the fruit of the light is goodness, righteousness, and truth, and is contrasted with the fruitless deeds of darkness. What does that mean?

What are Christians to do with the darkness?

What does it mean to 'find out what pleases the Lord'?

"Neither do people light a lamp and put it under a bowl. Instead they put it on its stand, and it gives light to everyone in the house." (Matthew 5:15) What are we to do with our light?

List below some of the ways you can let your light shine?

22. JOINT HEIRS WITH CHRIST

Though I am but flesh and blood
My life a passing flower,
In eternal time this life is brief
Like a summer shower.

And though I was but nothing
Upon Christ's payment, I did believe,
Now I've become joint-heirs with Christ
Eternal life in heaven to receive.

"The Spirit Himself testifies with our spirit that we are God's children. Now if we are children, then we are heirs – heirs of God and co-heirs with Christ, if indeed we share in His sufferings in order that we may also share in His glory." (Romans 8:16,17)

~ ~ ~ ~ ~

Life on earth is brief, and the older you are, the faster it seems time passes. Sometimes people put too much emphasis on accumulating wealth and putting their treasures on earth. The things that we have on earth will be left behind and will rot and rust away.

When we trust Christ as our savior, we are born in God's family and become children of God. Eternal life is a gift of God, a purchased possession by the precious blood of Christ.

The Bible says that when we do things in Christ's name, we will receive rewards in heaven. When we store our treasures in heaven, they will be there waiting for us. There we will see Jesus face to face and spend eternity with Him. We will be able to dwell in His love and be filled with His light.

When we trust Jesus as our savior, we are sealed by the Holy Spirit. This seal means that we belong to God, and we are His child. What does it mean that we become heirs of God?

There is nothing wrong with having nice things on earth. List some of the treasures you have upon earth.

Do you also have treasures in heaven? Which is more critical, treasures on earth or in heaven?

When compared to what we will be like in heaven, we are all suffering on this earth. What are some of the ways you are suffering?

Do you think that all this suffering will be worth it when we see Jesus in heaven?

No matter what we are going through on earth, good times or not, our life on earth is fleeting. Are you looking forward to seeing Jesus one day?

23. GOD'S PROVISIONS

Some people live their lives believing,
   Whatever they have they've earned,
The harder they work, the more they have
   Whatever is given out is returned.

But they are forgetting one great fact,
   That everything comes from above,
God gives us health and food on our table,
   And showers us with His love.

Jesus said, "I am the vine; you are the branches. If you remain in me and I in you, you will bear much fruit; apart from me you can do nothing...If you remain (abide) in me and my words remain (abide) in you, ask whatever you wish, and it will be done for you. This is to my Father's glory, that you bear much fruit, showing yourselves to be my disciples". (John 15:5,7-8)

~ ~ ~ ~ ~

God created us to glorify and praise Him. We aren't to boast about all the wealth we have accumulated on earth, or our beauty or degrees. It is nice to have those things, but they are not to be first in our life.

Bearing fruit and glorifying God is the ultimate purpose of being a Christian. We can only bear fruit when we are connected to Christ and get our strength through Him. This 'abiding in Christ' is a close intimate relationship with Him, and through Christ, we bear fruit.

"But the fruit of the Spirit is love, joy, peace, forbearance, kindness, goodness, faithfulness, gentleness, and self-control.

Against such things there is no law." (Galatians 5:22,23) Bearing fruit brings glory to God.

Christ is the _____ and we are the _____.

The verses above state that a few things happen to us when we abide in Christ. Write them in the space below.

When we abide in Christ, we bear fruit. What are some of the fruit we bear?

The poem mentions that some people think that everything comes from themselves. What is your opinion?

Who do we get our blessings from?

What does 'abide in Christ' mean to you?

24. A MISSIONARY

I am not rich by standards
In fact, I'm really quite poor,
My body grows weary from toiling
My feet from walking are sore.

Though it seems I have nothing,
My riches in heaven are placed,
Even if I had riches on earth
Only those in heaven would last.

"How, then, can they call on the one they have not believed in? And how can they believe in the one of whom they have not heard? And how can they hear without someone preaching to them? And how can they preach unless they are sent? As it is written, 'How beautiful are the feet of those who bring good news!'" (Romans 10:14,15)

~ ~ ~ ~ ~

Jesus died on the cross to pay for all sin, but a person has to believe in His payment to be saved. People cannot believe in something that they haven't heard. Winning souls is active. We have to talk to others and back up our witnessing with a life pleasing to Jesus.

God has called some to be missionaries to other countries where they can share the gospel to the unsaved. Even though we might not be a missionary, there are people in our communities and neighborhoods that need to hear the gospel.

Living a good life is important, but talking about Christ is what saves people. Let our feet be the ones that bring the gospel to others.

We consider missionaries as people who are called by God and sent out by the local church as a witness of the gospel. Are you now, or have you ever wanted to be a missionary?

What is your opinion of missionaries? Should they only go overseas, or can they be missionaries in their homeland?

What is your opinion of financially supporting missionaries or mission groups?

God wants everyone to be saved, but they have to hear the gospel to trust Christ as their Savior. Should we leave it up to others?

Have you ever shared the gospel of Jesus' death on the cross for our sins to someone else?

What do the verses above say about someone who shares the gospel?

25. BURDEN OF MY YOUTH

God, I come in prayer tonight,
    And open up my heart.
This heavy burden upon my soul
    Is tearing me apart.

When I was young, not long ago
    Warnings I did not heed.
In my folly, I went astray
    Upon pleasures, I did feed.

This but one mistake I made
    Was built upon the sand,
And like the cliffs by the sea
    It will always stand.

My life is still before me,
    Starting over cannot be done.
My prayer is not to erase the past
    Or from my life to run.

But like the ocean on the beach,
    Slowly washes the sand away,
Please fade this burden in my heart
    Until it's gone one day.

"He does not treat us as our sins deserve or repay us according to our iniquities. For as high as the heavens are above the earth so great is His love for those who fear Him; as far as the east is from the west, so far has He removed our transgressions from us." (Psalms 103:10-12)

~ ~ ~ ~ ~

We are all sinners, and we do things that we wish we hadn't done. We may have done things that have long term consequences, and it can be a reminder of our past mistake. We may forgive others of wrongs against us, but sometimes we have trouble forgiving ourselves of things we have done.

When Christ died on the cross, He made a complete payment for our sins. When we accept Him as our Savior, all our sins are forgiven, which includes past, present, and future sins, large and small.

To have emotional peace, we are not to live in the past and keep wishing we could change the past. Contentment is accepting how things are now. When God says He forgives us of our sins as far as the east is from the west, they are gone from us. We need to accept what God says and live in His comfort.

We all make mistakes. Some are bigger than others. Have you ever done something in your life that you wish you hadn't done?

Is there something you did wrong in your past, that is still bothering you?

What does the verse above say about God forgiving us of our sins? If God forgives us, should we forgive ourselves?

Forgiving ourselves of something we did wrong is not the same things as forgetting it happened. We know it happened, but it doesn't hold any power over us any longer. Are you able to forgive yourself for the mistakes you made? Why or Why not?

Some people say that they made mistakes in their past, and through it, they have become a better person. Do you agree or disagree with this statement?

If you are still bothered by something in your past, what steps should be done to help you live in the present?

26. JONATHAN'S JOURNEY

Our God in the heavens
  Only he knows,
In this great country
  Where Jonathan goes.

He's on a journey
  From the east to the west
The sky is his window,
  The ground is his rest.

And while he is gone,
  To God, I will pray,
That He keeps him safely
  And blesses his way.

"I have not stopped giving thanks for you, remembering you in my prayers." (Ephesians 1:16)

~ ~ ~ ~ ~

We have friends and neighbors that we have known for years, and then they move away. When our close friends are called into the mission field, and we won't see them for years at a time, we feel sad. Sometimes our children will grow up and go away to college, or move out of state for a job opportunity, and we feel left behind.

God will bring preachers or other people into our paths that can minister to us, and we develop a close bond with them. Then God calls them away to another field where they can minister to others.

When we are separated from our loved ones, it is a great comfort to know that God is watching over and taking care of them. We can daily pray for their safety and wellbeing. Sometimes we know that the parting is only temporarily, and other times we don't know if we will meet again. The memories we share and how we touched each other's lives will always be with us.

The older we are, the more people have moved in and out of our lives. Name some of the non-relative people that have meant the most to you.

How did these people help you on your journey in life?

The verse above says we should pray for others. Why should we pray for others?

Have you ever been out camping and slept under the stars and moonlight?

To some people being out in nature makes them feel closer to God. What are your thoughts?

When we are living close to our family members, or if they have moved away, we should always pray to God for them, that He showers us all with His blessings.

27. THE WORD LOVE

To some people love is just a word,
   That's easy for them to say,
Because it doesn't mean much to them
   They use it to get their way.

Others never say it at all,
   Because to them, it's understood,
And we know this is also wrong
   To speak it often they should.

To me, love is not just a word
   But of feelings from the soul,
And to those who give and receive it
   It makes their being whole.

And even though I've told you before
   In many different ways,
I'll love you with all my heart
   All my life long days.

"I pray that out of His glorious riches He may strengthen you with power through His Spirit in your inner being, so that Christ may dwell in your hearts through faith. And I pray that you, being rooted and established in love, may have power, together with all the Lord's holy people, to grasp how wide and long and high and deep is the love of Christ, and to know this love that surpasses knowledge – that you may be filled to the measure of all the fullness of God." (Ephesians 3:16-19)

~ ~ ~ ~ ~

When we trust Christ as our Savior, we are immediately indwelled with the Holy Spirit, and Christ is dwelling in us. We are the temple of the Holy Spirit, and we are to give our bodies as a living sacrifice to God.

Do we only show love to our family and friends with words? We are to also show our love with deeds and actions. Through prayer and faith, we are to put Christ first in our lives. To know Christ, we are to keep His commandments and abide in Him. When we are grounded in Christ as a tree planted by the spiritual waters of life, then we can begin to experience the love of Christ.

"Out of His glorious riches," what does that mean to you?

According to the verses above, who dwells within our hearts? Who are we strengthened with through power?

According to the poem, what makes our being whole?

The apostle Paul prayed that we might be rooted and established in the love of Christ. What does that mean to you?

Can you explain what it means to be filled to the measure of the fullness of God?

To some people, the word 'love' comes quickly out of their mouths, and they say it all the time. What does the word 'love' mean to you?

28. NATURE

N ature is all around us

A bounding ever so

T rees are into forests –

U nderneath flowers grow

      And a

R ighteous God protects

E verything, you know.

"Then God said, 'I give you every seed-bearing plant on the face of the whole earth and every tree that has fruit with seed in it. They will be yours for food. And to all the beasts of the earth and all the birds in the sky and all the creatures that move along the ground – everything that has the breath of life in it – I give every green plant for food.' And it was so. God saw all that He had made, and it was very good. And there was evening, and there was morning – the sixth day." (Genesis 1:29-31)

~ ~ ~ ~ ~

The Bible states that God created the heavens and earth in six days and that everything was created out of nothing. God spoke them into being. After His creation, God said that what He created was good.

God reveals Himself to us through nature and the Bible. When we look at rivers, lakes, and oceans, we see the handiwork of God. The clouds, rainbows, and sunsets paint the skies. Trees, plants, and animals are all designed by God. The rain that waters the earth so that plants can grow speaks of the creator's love and how He provides for us.

The Bible says that God created the heavens and earth in six days and that God created man. The schools teach evolution, and that we evolved from the Big Bang or some other theory. What is your opinion about creation?

Which do you think came first, the chicken or the egg? LOL

God said that He created everything and that it was good. What are your thoughts?

The Bible says that the heavens are the handiwork of God. Do you enjoy looking at a sunrise or sunset, or the clouds floating in the sky?

There are parks and nature trails where we can see nature. Do you enjoy walking in the woods or on nature trails?

God created mountains, streams, rivers, oceans, flowers, birds, and much more for us to enjoy. Where are some of the places that you have been that show God's handiwork?

29. FACING REALITY

To look into our life
  And face reality,
We cannot look too hard,
  For fear of what we'll see.

We need to coat our vision,
  With a plan and dream,
And being optimistic
  Easier, our life will seem.

"Though the fig tree does not bud and there are no grapes on the vines, though the olive crop fails and the fields produce no food, though there are no sheep in the pen and no cattle in the stalls, yet I will rejoice in the Lord, I will be joyful in God my Savior." (Habakkuk 3:17,18)

~ ~ ~ ~ ~

We may go through life thinking we are doing fine, and everything is great. If we happen to stop and think about how life really is, are we satisfied with ourselves? Some people might realize that they are shallow and not like what they see. Some people stay busy because they know that their life isn't as favorable as they portray it to be, and pretend that they are fine.

The test would come if we lost everything, would we still be content and happy? Is our life based upon what we have?

When a person bases their life upon God, then they can be content in whatever circumstances they are in. True peace and joy come from within the person, not from without. When we are depending and trusting in God to take care of us, then we have a future that is bright.

The poem alludes to the fact that we are all sinners saved by grace. Dwelling too much on the negative aspects of ourselves can cause depression. What are your thoughts about dwelling too much on the negative in life?

What circumstances and things in life cause you to be optimistic?

In what ways does being optimistic in life help our emotional health?

The verses above are saying that even though we don't have much in life, we can still rejoice in the Lord. Why should we rejoice in the Lord?

Why does our happiness not depend upon what we have, but in trusting in God, and having a personal relationship with Him?

How does being optimistic and rejoicing in the Lord go hand in hand?

30. CHOOSE YOUR FRIENDS

A friend is like a path,
They can lead you right or wrong,
They can tear your values down,
Or help you be more strong.

A friend's words throw weight
Upon what you think or do,
So when you pick your friends
Think of their effect on you.

Will your friend help you grow
In morals and in the Lord,
For if they bring you down
Their friendship you can't afford.

So pray to God to send you
Good friends to walk beside,
And give you the courage
To cast others on the side.

"So Jonathan made a covenant with the house of David, saying, 'May the Lord call David's enemies to account.' And Johnathan had David reaffirm his oath out of love for him, because he loved him as he loved himself." (1 Samuel 20:16,17)

~ ~ ~ ~ ~

God had chosen Saul be the first king in Israel, but He wasn't pleased with Saul because he disobeyed what God wanted him to do. God said that David would be the next king in Israel, and not Saul's children, which would be Jonathan. Jonathan knew he wouldn't be king and still loved David as his friend.

In those times, a king would often kill all the children of the former king to make their kingship secure. After King Saul and Jonathan were killed in battle and David became king, he sought out Jonathan's son, Mephibosheth, and said that he would always eat at his table.

David and Jonathan were true friends and helped each other. We all have the desire to have friends, but we need to be careful of the friends we have in our inner circle. We need friends that will help us grow spiritually in the Lord.

King Saul was jealous of David and wanted him dead. In spite of that, what kind of friendship did David and Jonathan have?

How did David and Jonathan show their friendship to each other?

In what ways did David help Jonathan's son, Mephibosheth?

There are many types of friendships. Some people are best friends, some friends, and others acquaintances. Some can be coworkers or classmates. Who are some of your closest friends? What part do they play in your life?

Our closest friends have a significant influence on us. What should you do if you have friends that do not help you spiritually?

How can you be a good friend to others?

31. MY CAT

Of all the animals in the land
   I think my cats the best,
And because she's in my life
   I am so very blessed.

Early in the morning
   She jumps up on my feet,
And then we play together
   Until it's time to eat.

Sometimes when I'm sad,
   And can't go out to play,
She lays upon my lap
   And brightens up my day.

And when the day is over,
   And I'm tucked inside my bed,
She purrs goodnight to me,
   And sleeps beside my head.

"And God said, 'Let the land produce living creatures according to their kinds: the livestock, the creatures that move along the ground, and the wild animals, each according to its kind.' And it was so. God made the wild animals according to their kinds, the livestock according to their kinds, and all the creatures that move along the ground according to their kinds. And God saw that it was good." (Genesis 1:24,25)

~ ~ ~ ~ ~

The livestock that God created includes cats, dogs, and other creatures that are our pets. God said that the animals he created were good. If God cares for His animals, then so should we.

Cats and pets are created by God and are a blessing from Him. Parents will give their children pets to teach them responsibility. The universe depends upon God to take care of it, so pets depend upon their owners to take care of them.

Pets provide companionship and love in our lives. When we have had a bad day, being with our pets lifts our spirits.

"The wolf will live with the lamb, the leopard will lie down with the goat, the calf and the lion and the yearling together; and a little child will lead them." (Isaiah 11:6) The Bible says that during the Millennial reign of Christ, this will happen. Wouldn't it be nice to be able to lay down with a big tiger or lion?

Have you ever had any pets in your life? What kind?

Do you have any pets now?

Sometimes parents will give their children pets to take care of to teach them responsibility. What is your experience or opinion about that?

They say that the elderly live longer when they have a pet to take care of. Pets may be beneficial to veterans and others with post-traumatic stress disorder. What is your opinion?

I think pets are fantastic and I am glad that God created them for us to enjoy!

32. GOODNIGHT PRAYER

Lord, I thank you for this day,
For the friends, you send my way,
And my family as they lay,
In their beds, now I pray.

Thank you for the Word I read
For the stories to take heed,
But most of all for Christ you gave,
Who died for me my soul to save.

Thank you, Lord. Amen.

"This, then, is how you should pray: 'Our Father in heaven, hallowed be Your name, Your kingdom come, Your will be done, on earth as it is in heaven. Give us today our daily bread. And forgive us our debts, as we also have forgiven our debtors. And lead us not into temptation but deliver us from the evil one.'" (Matthew 6:9-13)

~ ~ ~ ~ ~

The Lord's prayer is an example of how we should pray, not something repetitive to follow. God is represented as our Father and approachable to us. He is more interested in our communicating with Him from our heart than in the specific words we use.

As Christ died on the cross and paid for all our sins, we should also forgive those who sin against us.

All good things come from God, and He blesses those who follow Him. When we pray to God, we are acknowledging that He is our Father and that He is taking care of us. As we should eat every day to nourish our bodies, we also should read our Bibles and pray every day to nourish our souls.

Christ gave us the Lord's Prayer as an example of how to pray. Are you repetitive in your prayers, or do think about Jesus when you are praying?

God answers our prayers in three ways: yes, no, and wait. When we pray in His will, we need to accept the answer that He gives us. Do you pray in God's will?

Sometimes we might not like God's answer to our prayers. Are you able to accept God's answers?

Sometimes we get busy in our lives and forget to thank the Lord for the things He has provided for us. What are some of the things you can praise the Lord for?

The Bible says we should pray for others. Who are some of the people you can pray for?

We have salvation by accepting the payment that Christ made on the cross for us. We should thank the Lord daily for saving our souls and giving us the free gift of eternal life.

33. DAILY READ GOD'S WORD

Too busy in my life I was
To read God's word every day,
My many friends and commitments
Took me from the Lord to stray.

And when I got in trouble
Not a way out I could see,
Then I turned to God for help
And, by His grace, He helped me.

For through the Bible we learn
True life and how to live,
And if we follow carefully
Blessings to us, God will give.

"Jesus answered, "It is written: 'Man shall not live on bread alone, but on every word that comes from the mouth of God.'" (Matthew 4:4)

~ ~ ~ ~ ~

Do you ever feel like you are living in the wilderness? No matter how hard you try, things don't seem to work out? Grumbling and complaining are how we often handle situations that bring us discomfort. The children of Israel went through the wilderness, and they continually complained and did not appreciate what the Lord was doing or had done for them. They complained when they didn't have any food.

God sent them manna in the morning to be food for them, and they had to gather it six days out of the week. The children of Israel had to collect their food daily or they couldn't eat.

The Bible equips us to be able to serve God and shows us how to live our lives on earth so that we can glorify Him. The Word of God explains how we, as humans, can have a relationship with Jesus. As the children of Israel gathered manna to feed their body daily, we should read God's Word daily to feed our souls.

Sometimes we may feel lost in life, and things aren't working out for us. Do you ever feel like you are living in the wilderness?

When the Children of Israel were hungry, how did they react?

Sometimes we grumble and complain when things don't go our way. What should we be doing instead?

Why does the Bible tell us that we are not to live on bread alone, but on every word that comes from the mouth of God?

In what ways do we benefit from reading the Bible?

"Oh, how I love your law! I meditate on it all day long." (Psalms 119:97) What are your thoughts?

34. THOUGHTS BEFORE MARRIAGE

So many people say they're in love,
   But all they do is fight,
Ups and downs, emotional rounds
   This can't be quite right.

Two people can say they're in love,
   And maybe they think they are,
Emotional trips and games they play,
   Their love lacks much by far.

True love is when someone puts,
   The other first in their life,
True love is a bond of peace
   Wherein there is no strife.

So, if you think you're in love,
   And your life is turned inside out,
Reconsider the mess you're in
   And start looking round about.

For there is someone out there
   Who'll love you with all his heart,
He'll be kind and treat you well,
   Find him and never part.

"A quarrelsome wife is like the dripping of a leaky roof in a rainstorm; restraining her is like restraining the wind or grasping oil with the hand. (Proverbs 27:15,16)

~ ~ ~ ~ ~

A quarrelsome person can apply equally to men and women. Sometimes when people "fall in love," their emotions take over, and they may "overlook" numerous negative qualities in the other person. The Bible states that we are not to be "unequally yoked" with an unbeliever, which means Christians are not to date or marry unbelievers and would cause numerous problems in the relationship.

A contentious man or woman's actions cause a negative atmosphere over everyone around them. They are a constant frustration, like a leaky roof that does not stop dripping. God wants marriage to last a lifetime and living a life with an argumentative spouse is to be avoided.

God wants us to have peace in our marriages. If you are arguing too much with the person, consider breaking up. Waiting is better than a bad marriage.

The poem is talking about people who are not married and are having lots of arguments. Why do you think people get married when they are already having problems in their relationship?

The best predictor of future behavior is past behavior. What should a couple do if they say they love each other, want to marry, but are often arguing?

Love is an emotion, and our emotions may play tricks on us. We also can make excuses for what we do. What are your thoughts?

"Trust in the Lord with all your heart and lean not on your own understanding; in all your ways submit to Him, and He will make your paths straight." (Proverbs 3:5,6) Who are we to trust with our emotions?

When we are on crooked paths, we may stumble and fall. What kind of path does God create for us?

What kind of path do you want for your life?

35. TOGETHERNESS

T ogether

O ften

G iving

E ncouragement

T houghtfully

H elping

E veryone.

R ejoicing

N ightly

E ncouraging

S ouls

S haring.

"May the God who gives endurance and encouragement give you the same attitude of mind toward each other that Christ Jesus had, so that with one mind and one voice you may glorify the God and Father of our Lord Jesus Christ. Accept one another, then, just as Christ accepted you, in order to bring praise to God." (Romans 15:5-7)

~ ~ ~ ~ ~

Many different passages in the Bible tell us to encourage one another. Christ told his disciples that in this world, we would have troubles, but do not be discouraged because He overcame the world. As God is patient and comforts us, He also wants us to come alongside and comfort others.

Life can become difficult, and we may want to give up. When a friend comes alongside and gives us words of comfort and reassurance, they share our burden and give meaning to our lives. No man is an island, and we are all brothers and sisters in Christ. Jesus wants us to encourage and help one another. Encouraging one another makes it easier for us to live the Christian life and brings Glory to God.

The verse above speaks about us having the same attitude of mind for each other that Christ has for us. What do you think is the attitude that God wants us to have?

Accepting others as Christ accepts us means that we should look at others as Christ sees them. If we do that, do you think it will change some people's opinions of others?

What do we bring to God when we encourage and accept others?

In the book of Acts, a Levite from Cyprus whose name was Joseph was nicknamed Barnabas, which means "son of encouragement" (Acts 4:36,37) because he helped others. Do you know of anyone who you feel is a "Barnabas"?

The Bible also speaks of Barnabas as a "good man, full of the Holy Spirit and faith." Barnabas allowed the Holy Spirit to work through him. When we are led by the Spirit, we also can accomplish great things.

In what ways can you encourage others?

36. CHILDREN ARE GOD'S GIFT

Children are God's gift to us,
    To use and mold for Him,
And with the birth of a child
    A new dawn is to begin.

"Children are a heritage from the Lord, offspring a reward from Him. Like arrows in the hands of a warrior are children born in one's youth. Blessed is the man whose quiver is full of them." (Psalms 127:3-5a)

~ ~ ~ ~ ~

The Bible says that children are a blessing from God.

Some people might feel that their child is not a blessing from God because of the circumstances surrounding their birth or other events. The Bible says that God loves us and has plans for each of us. When we look at each child as God sees them, then we can understand that they are a blessing from God.

God gives parents the responsibility to raise their children according to the word of God. We are to teach them love and respect for one another and love and respect for the Lord.

Children are innocent and trusting. They teach us patience and understanding. When it is all said and done, they are worth it, and a blessing from God.

Why would some people think that their child is not a blessing from God?

Would that thinking reflect how they treat their child?

The Bible says that we are all created in the image of God, which gives us value. What do the verses above say about children?

"Where there are no oxen, the manger is empty, but from the strength of an ox come abundant harvests." (Proverbs 14:4). Reflect on the fact that when there are no children in the home, there aren't any toys lying around, but with children comes the mess. What are some of the abundant harvests the verse may be speaking about?

What is a parent's part in God's plan for each child?

If you have children, what are some of the blessings you have received from them?

37. THIS EARTHLY RACE

Lord, give me the faith to see
  And wisdom to understand,
That the future is to be lived
  As You have wisely planned.

Lord, give me the peace inside,
  That comes from trusting You,
Through You to live each day
  In everything I do.

Lord, help me keep my eyes above,
  My riches in heaven to place,
So that with joy I may run,
  This earthly human race.

"Do you not know that in a race all the runners run, but only one gets the prize? Run in such a way as to get the prize. Everyone who competes in the games goes into strict training. They do it to get a crown that will not last, but we do it to get a crown that will last forever. Therefore I do not run like someone running aimlessly; I do not fight like a boxer beating the air. No, I strike a blow to my body and make it my slave so that after I have preached to others, I myself will not be disqualified for the prize." (1 Corinthians 9: 24-27)

~ ~ ~ ~ ~

The Bible describes the Christian life as running in a race. To be a competitive runner, the athlete must discipline their body, train, and sacrifice to run and win the prize.

In the Christian life, we must discipline ourselves and be focused on serving Christ and putting our treasures in heaven. We are to cast things aside that slow us down in running the race. God created us to glorify Him, and everything we do should be to please God and bring glory to Him. Then we will receive a crown that will last in heaven.

The verses above say that Christians are running in a race. What kind of competition are we running?

What are some of the things we should do to be able to compete well in the race?

Should we run aimlessly? How should we run?

What kind of a crown did the people competing in Paul's day receive?

If we compete in the race the way that God wants us to, what will we receive when we get to heaven?

The verses above say that we are to stay focused on running the race for eternal rewards. Are you willing to compete in God's race?

38. WISHES

I wish I were a millionaire,
   With a Rolls Royce at my door,
Then I could ride in style
   From the mountains to the shore.

I wish I had a sable mink,
   To wear when it is cold,
And five walk-in closets
   For all my clothes to hold.

I wish I had three children,
   Who never ever fought,
Who always did what was told
   And never a cold was caught.

But wishes are like dreams,
   And in the morning fade away,
So, what I wish the most for
   Is to accept my life each day.

"I am not saying this because I am in need, for I have learned to be content whatever the circumstances. I know what it is to be in need, and I know what it is to have plenty. I have learned the secret of being content in any and every situation, whether well fed or hungry, whether living in plenty or in want. I can do all things through Christ who gives me strength." (Philippians 4:11-13)

~ ~ ~ ~ ~

A person could have extreme wealth and not be happy. A person could have very little and be satisfied. This is where contentment comes in, being happy with what we have. It is not to say if we are poor, we should not strive for a better job, or work harder for something we want, but in whatever circumstances we are in, appreciate what we have.

It is like the expression; 'do you see the cup half full or half empty?' It is not our circumstances, but our thoughts about our circumstances that make us content because things could always be worse. The Lord says that He will take care of us. We should daily pray to

God and give thanks for what He has given us and be content.

It is fine to wish for nice things, for instance, a vacation in Hawaii, or to own a cabin in the mountains. What are some of the things you wish for?

It is nice to have dreams like owning a home or graduating from college. What are some of the dreams you have?

Wanting nice things can become sin when we are consumed with them and become discontent with what we have. Rate on a scale 0 to 10 how content you are with your life right now.

Paul was content in all his circumstances. What are some of the events Paul went through?

We all go through hard times and difficult situations. What did you learn through your hard times?

In all circumstances, we should give praise to God. List some of the things in your life that have been blessings from God?

39. GIVE BURDENS TO GOD

When you're down and troubled
　And no one seems to care,
When you've got burdens on your heart
　And no one's there to share.

Then look above to God up high
　Who's always ready to hear,
Place your burdens in His care
　For God is always near.

"I have told you these things, so that in Me you may have peace. In this world you will have trouble. But take heart! I have overcome the world." (John 16:33)

~ ~ ~ ~ ~

Adam's sin has affected every facet of our being, and things now are not what God had intended them to be. Because of the fall, our bodies are afflicted by pain, suffering, and emotional problems, such as depression and anxiety.

There are outward problems such as calamities, hurricanes, tornadoes, and fires that destroy homes and property. There are also inward problems that affect our relationships with our husbands, wives, families, and friends.

We might feel alone in our troubles, but we are not alone. Christ said that when He went back up to heaven, He would send the Holy Spirit to guide and direct us. In the world, we have tribulations, but in Christ, we have peace. Christ is the true source of happiness which nothing can take away. When the storm is all around us, we are secure in God's love. True peace and joy come from following Jesus and having fellowship with Him, which no one can take from us.

Everyone goes through trials and tribulations in their life. What are some of the trials that you have endured?

Did you have someone come alongside you and help you through the storm?

Looking back, how did you handle the problems you faced?

In the verse above, Christ says that we will have troubles in this life. Why is that so?

Christ sent the Holy Spirit to be our comforter. The Holy Spirit is inside us to guide and direct us. What does that mean?

Are you going through trials now? If so, are you asking and praying for God to help you?

40. GOD'S BLESSINGS

The closer I've drawn to God
The more I'm able to see,
That God is a God of love
With blessings in store for me.

"This is love: not that we loved God, but that He loved us and sent His Son as an atoning sacrifice for our sins. Dear friends, since God so loved us, we also ought to love one another." (1 John 4:10,11)

~ ~ ~ ~ ~

Love is an attribute of God and is a core aspect of His character. Some of God's other attributes of holiness, righteousness, justice, and wrath do not conflict and are in harmony with His attribute of love. God is the perfect example of pure love and sent Jesus Christ to die on the cross for our sins to restore the broken relationship we have with Him because of our sin.

Through the Holy Spirit inside of us, we are able also to love others. God does not force us to love Him and others but has given us free will to choose to do so. When we live our lives based on His Word, then we can have fellowship with Him and receive blessings.

God's love is the source of His blessing to us. When we put God first in our lives and live for Him, then we can live the life God desires for us. Only God can bless us with peace, joy, and happiness that the world cannot know.

God is Love. What does that mean to you?

In the verse above, how did God show His love for us?

God sacrificed His Son on the cross for our sins. God wants us to love others. In what ways can you love others?

Little children take things for granted, for instance, a home to live in and food on the table. In the same way, how might we take God for granted?

When children mature, they understand what their parents do for them. What has God done for you?

Write below some of the blessings you have received from God.

41. LOVE IS LIKE A BUTTERFLY

Love is like a butterfly,
  Lighting here and there,
Very fickle in its flight
  With its love to share.

And like the butterfly,
  Lights many times a day,
In our lives, love touches us
  In many different ways.

So, do not be illusioned,
  Thinking love is what you're in,
'Cause tomorrow might bring another
  And your love will start again.

So, trust in God to help you see
  The one He has for you,
Where your souls can be one
  In a love that will be true.

"The Lord God said, 'It is not good for man to be alone. I will make a helper suitable for him...So the Lord God caused the man to fall into a deep sleep; and while he was sleeping, he took one of the man's ribs and then closed up the place with flesh. Then the Lord God made a woman from the rib he had taken out of the man, and He brought her to the man. The man said, 'This is now bone of my bones and flesh of my flesh; she shall be called 'woman,' for she was taken out of man. That is why a man leaves his father and mother and is united to his wife, and they become one flesh." (Genesis 2:18, 22-25)

~ ~ ~ ~ ~

God created Eve because Adam was lonely. The love that was designed for each other was not the love we have for brothers, sisters, friends, but that they would essentially become one. The Bible says that a man is to love his wife as Christ loves the church and gave Himself for it, and wives are to respect their husbands.

Marriage is a holy institution and should not be taken lightly. Carefully chose your partner in God's will, where you can have love and companionship.

Adam was the first man. Why did God create Eve?

If God created women to be a helper suitable to men, and the man is to love their wife as Christ loves the church, then why are there so many miserable marriages?

Looking back over your life, have you ever been in a miserable marriage or relationship?

God's plan is for a man and a woman to be complete in marriage, and God doesn't take the wedding vows lightly. That is why people should carefully consider the person that they want to marry. It is not God's plan that we are miserable in a marriage. What are some things that a person can do to feel comfortable that the person they are marrying is the Lord's will in their life?

They say opposites attract, but the more things a couple has in common, the better the chances are of a good marriage. Why do you think that is so?

Love affects us in many different ways. What are some of the different ways love has touched you?

42. MY THOUGHTS OF YOU

I thought of you again tonight,
　　While I was all alone,
The stars were twinkling in the sky
　　The moon so brightly shone.

And I called out to God above,
　　To hear my heartfelt plea,
To keep you safely in His care
　　And bring you back to me.

"It was also called Mizpah, because he said, 'May the Lord keep watch between you and me when we are away from each other." (Genesis 31:49)

~ ~ ~ ~ ~

Jacob spent 20 years working for his father in law, Laban, but things didn't turn out well, and he fled quickly with his wives and children to go to his home country. When Laban found out Jacob left, he was upset and went after him with his men. At night, God spoke to Laban and told him not to say anything good or bad to Jacob. When Jacob and Laban met, there was contention between them, but they came to an amicable agreement. The place has since been called Mizpah.

The original use of the word Mizpah meant 'safeguard and warning' and has changed over time to be a 'beacon or watchtower.' God is our watchtower watching over us when we are separated from one another.

When adult children go away to college, or leave home and move to other states, or siblings move away, then it is comforting to know that

God is watching over them. We pray that God will keep everyone safe until we can meet face to face again.

Sometimes spouses or family members will go away on business or extended vacations. Do you have a family member that is away from you now?

Do you have any adult children that are away to college, or have moved to another state?

How do you feel about your family member not being close to you?

Laban was angry that Joseph left and wanted to do him harm, but God kept him from doing so. What was the original meaning of Mizpah, and how do we use it today?

God wants us to live peacefully with everyone, if possible. If you have relatives that you are not speaking to, is there something you can do to restore the relationship?

God is our watchtower, and our strength in time of need. Praying for those who are away from us and trusting in God's protection will calm our anxieties.

43. STARTING OVER

While we're passing through this life
   We make friends along the way,
We have our jobs and families
   To take up all our day.

One by one our friends are gone,
   And, our lives are broken up,
Our jobs have changed and, we move on,
   By ourselves each night we sup.

Then we sit and realize
   It's a crossroad that we've found,
That the past is left behind
   No ties to us are bound.

The future again looks bright,
   On the new road, we will find,
New friends and new commitments
   As those, we left behind.

"Therefore, if anyone is in Christ, the new creation has come. The old has gone, the new is here." (2 Corinthians 5:17)

~ ~ ~ ~ ~

When we trust Christ as our savior, we are born again, and become a new creation in Christ. Before our unregenerate heart was filled with enmity against God. Now we are reconciled to Him and are a child of God.

Even Christians can be addicted to substances, alcohol, and other ways of life that are against what God desires for us. They grab ahold of us and are difficult to overcome. When a person realizes that they need to change their life, they should let go of their negative habits and start a new life.

Starting over can be difficult because they will have to leave some of their customs and friends behind and start over with new friends and beginnings. Christ is there to help us along the way. The Holy Spirit inside will guide and direct us to become the person that we want to be. We can have peace in our lives that the world cannot give because we are new creations in Christ.

Life is unpredictable. People come and go, and our circumstances change. Have you been through situations that weren't good for you?

What were those circumstance, and how did you change? Was it difficult for you?

Are you now going through difficulties, or have things in your life that you know aren't right for you?

Sometimes we have friends that are not a good influence on us, and we should distance ourselves from them. Do you have any friends in your life that you feel shouldn't be there?

God wants what is best for us, and we want to be in His will. Sometimes we have to let things go and start over. Are there things in your life that you need to let go and start over?

What steps should you do to start over and become the person that you want to be?

44. CHRISTMAS TREE

Christmas tree
All shimmering bright,
Lights sparkling
Into the night.
Memories past
Filtering out,
Thoughts anew
Drifting about.
Thoughts anew
Drifting about.

"While they were there, the time came for the baby to be born, and she gave birth to her firstborn, a son. She wrapped Him in cloths and placed Him in a manger, because there was no guest room available for them. And there were shepherds living out in the fields nearby, keeping watch over their flocks at night. An angel of the Lord appeared to them, and the glory of the Lord shone around them, and they were terrified. But the angel said to them, 'Do not be afraid. I bring you good news that will cause great joy for all the people. Today in the town of David a Savior has been born to you; He is the Messiah, the Lord.'" (Luke 2:6-11)

~ ~ ~ ~ ~

The baby that was born in the manger was God in the flesh, the Messiah. It was prophesied in the Old Testament that the Messiah would come, and when he was born, Angels proclaimed His birth.

We celebrate Christmas to remember the birth of Jesus. As the Maji gave gifts to Jesus, so we give gifts to each other in celebration of

Christ's birth. Memories are made and shared during the Christmas holiday.

The birth of Jesus was a significant event on earth and in time. Where was Jesus born?

The shepherds were afraid at first. What did the angel of the Lord say to the shepherds?

What does it mean that Christ is the Messiah?

Why do Christians celebrate Christmas?

To some people, Christmas is a time of joy, and to others, it is a time of sorrow? What would be some reasons why?

Christmas means different things to different people. What does Christmas mean to you?

45. GIVE PROBLEMS TO GOD

Life is a maze of twists and turns
And things don't turn out right,
Through trying we seem helpless
In battles and dreams, we fight.

Something I wanted is gone
And another has taken its place,
Dreams and illusions, it seems
Like butterflies in meadows, we chase.

But in life, I finally learned
These problems to God I will give,
He'll see things will turn out right
And my life will be easy to live.

"Blessed is the one who does not walk in step with the wicked or stand in the way that sinners take or sit in the company of mockers, but whose delight is in the law of the Lord, and who meditates on His law day and night. That person is like a tree planted by streams of water, which yields its fruit in season and whose leaf does not wither – whatever they do prospers." (Pslams1:1-3)

~ ~ ~ ~ ~

Life can seem confusing, and sometimes we don't know which direction we should go. It might be when things aren't turning out right, it is because we aren't living the way God wants us to, and we feel frustrated. God says we are not to participate in the vanity of life, nor participate in their works.

In our troubled times, we need to look to God for guidance and meditate on His word. Then we will be planted beside God's living waters. We will become like trees, which are stable and strong. We must grow and be mature before we can bear fruit. The waters that we draw from are refreshing and bring peace and joy to our lives. When we are serving God, whatever we do will prosper.

Are you going through a maze of twists and turns in life and don't know what to do?

Do you feel like you are chasing illusions or dreams?

Who are we to turn to when we have problems in life?

The verses above say that we are not to listen to ungodly counsel, but to meditate on God's word. Why is that important?

When we are planted next to the stream of God's living waters, what happens to us?

When we meditate on God's Word, we grow spiritually, and we produce fruit that can help others. Pause and reflect on this.

46. GOD WANTS ME

I have not much to offer
Life's not been good to me,
I have not fame and fortune
In fact, I'm poor, you see.

I saw life passing me by
My youth I cannot regain,
Every day was like the other
Every face I met the same.

Christ came and spoke to me
He wiped my tears with His hand,
"I've chosen you to follow me
Out of thousands in the land."

I gave my life to the Lord
Because He wants all of me.
He'll use me for His purpose
Whatever that may be.

"As He went along, He saw a man blind from birth. His disciples asked Him, 'Rabbi, who sinned, this man or his parents, that he was born blind?' 'Neither this man nor his parents sinned,' said Jesus, 'but this happened so that the works of God might be displayed in him.'" (John 9:1-3)

~ ~ ~ ~ ~

It is human nature to correlate negative circumstances with sin and positive circumstances with doing good. It is sometimes easy for people to think that when something bad happens to a person that there is sin in their life.

Because of the Fall, sin entered into the world, and our bodies, souls, and spirits are all affected by sin. We now have sickness and diseases, and humanity can be cruel and evil towards one another instead of loving and kind. Because we live in a sinful world, negative things happen to us.

Jesus said that the man was born blind, not because of his or his parent's sin, but because of a higher purpose of God. In our trials and tribulations, Christ wants us to draw near to

Him. He wants us to take our eyes off of this world and focus our minds on Him.

When something terrible happens to someone, do you sometimes think that they must have done something wrong for it to have happened?

Judging others can be an easy thing to do, but should we? We are all created by God, and He is the one who we will stand before one day.

The verse above states that the man born blind was for the glory of God. Reflect on that concept.

Job in the Bible lost everything he had in one day except for his wife. What is your opinion on bad things happening to good people?

God gave each one of us different talents, some more and some less. What are some of the ways God has blessed you?

In what ways can you live your life for the glory of God?

47. GOD'S CHRISTIAN

Lord, I look back on my day
And know I've failed again,
I always try to be so good
But something comes up, and then...

And so, I pray again tonight
To help me tomorrow to be,
The kind of Christian that you want,
And the type that I want to be.

"In the same way, count yourselves dead to sin but alive to God in Christ Jesus. Therefore do not let sin reign in your mortal body so that you obey its evil desires. Do not offer any part of yourself to sin as an instrument of wickedness, but rather offer yourselves to God as those who have been brought from death to life; and offer every part of yourself to Him as an instrument of righteousness. For sin shall no longer be your master, because you are not under the law, but under grace." (Romans 6:11-14)

~ ~ ~ ~ ~

Because Adam and Eve sinned, we are all born with a sin nature. In Romans 7:14-25 Paul is talking about how the old nature in us wants us to sin and disobey God. When we trust Christ as our savior, we receive a new nature that wants to please Him. The Bible says that even the most spiritual Christian has a battle inside to sin or to serve Jesus.

We are human, and we will not be delivered from sin until we are in heaven. We don't have to fight this constant battle alone.

The Holy Spirit is inside to guide us and direct us so that we may have a victorious life in Jesus.

All of us do things that we don't want to do because of the sin nature in us. What are some of the sins that you would like removed from your life?

Some people think that when they sin, Satan made them do it. Do you believe Satan made us sin, or we sin just because we are human beings?

We live in a world that is controlled by Satan. Do you think we sin because of the worldly influences around us?

Noah was a just man who lived in a very sinful world, and he survived through the flood. How do you think you would have handled living in Noah's time?

God is a forgiving God and forgives us from our sins. Every day is a new day, and we can start again. What do you think of that comment?

What kind of Christian do you want to be?

48. BURDEN FOR THE LOST

Lord help me to have
A burden for the lost,
That I will win souls
No matter the cost.

"Don't you have a saying, 'It's still four months until harvest'? I tell you, open your eyes and look at the fields! They are ripe for harvest. Even now the one who reaps draws a wage and harvests a crop for eternal life, so that the sower and the reaper may be glad together. Thus the saying 'One sows and another reaps' is true. I sent you to reap what you have not worked for. Others have done the hard work, and you have reaped the benefits of their labor." (John 4:35-38)

~ ~ ~ ~ ~

Sharing the gospel with others about how Christ died on the cross for our sins is not something that we should put off.

Some people may be attending church, or are searching for God, and want to trust Christ, but haven't heard the truth yet. They are ripe and are wanting to trust Christ. You don't have to wait to be a missionary to talk to others about Jesus; there are many unsaved people among each of us. All Christians should be soul winners for Christ. Just open up your eyes and look around at the harvest.

In the verses above, Christ was talking to His disciples. What did Christ say about the harvest?

There are many types of harvests. What harvest was Christ talking about?

What did Christ mean when He told his disciples that they are to harvest what others sowed?

Some people feel that they don't have the spiritual gift of soul winning and leave it up to others. Should everyone have a burden for the lost? Why or why not?

Do you believe that missionaries in other countries may be risking their lives to share the gospel?

Are you willing to reap in God's harvest?

49. THE FUTURES NOT KNOWN

As much as I wish it could
The futures not to be known,
I agonize over things
That are yet to be shown.

But it's God's way of saying
You have to trust in Me,
That I will take care of you
Relax and wait patiently.

"Do not be anxious about anything, but in every situation, by prayer and petition, with thanksgiving, present your requests to God. And the peace of God, which transcends all understanding, will guard your hearts and your minds in Christ Jesus." (Philippians 4:6,7)

~ ~ ~ ~ ~

It is easy to worry about things in our life, especially things we feel that we have no control over. We all have problems, but we don't have to bear them alone. The Bible tells us that when we are anxious, we should bring all of our needs and problems to God in prayer. God is concerned about everything that happens to us, and He wants to help us.

Prayer is the remedy for anxiety, and we are to bring our fears to God. When we turn our problems over to Him, then we have the peace of God in our souls that transcends all understanding. It is a peace that the world does not comprehend. We are to be thankful for all that the Lord has done for us, to Him who gives us peace. When we give our anxieties to God, then we can rest in His faithfulness.

Because we are all human, we all have some stress in our lives now and then. A little anxiety is sometimes useful; for example, it will help us study harder for a test. What are your thoughts?

Too much anxiety is not good, and it can create health problems. What are some of the things that you may be anxious about?

On an anxiety scale of 0 to 10, where 10 is very anxious, and 0 is not anxious at all, where do you feel you fall on the scale, overall?

The verses above say that we are to bring our requests with prayer and thanksgiving to God. Why should we do both?

God allows trials to come into our lives so we can trust in Him to help us. Are you trusting in God to help you?

According to the verses above, what does God give those who trust in Him?

50. THE SEA SHORE

I love hunting seashells,
  Early at the shore,
When the sun is rising
  I love to explore.

Some of the shells are common,
  They are found everywhere,
Some of the shells are treasures
  And extremely rare.

I love to hear the ocean waves,
  Breaking everywhere,
And to see the seagulls
  Flying in the air.

And when I'm home again,
  The shore is left behind,
I put the shells to my ear, and,
  I'm back there in my mind.

"God is our refuge and strength, an ever-present help in trouble. Therefore we will not fear, though the earth give way and the mountains fall into the heart of the sea, though its waters roar and foam and the mountains quake with their surging... He says, 'Be still, and know that I am God; I will be exalted among the nations, I will be exalted in the earth.'" (Psalms 46:1-3,10)

~ ~ ~ ~ ~

The context above is talking about King David being in a war, and in the midst, God says, "Be still, and know that I am God." God is our refuge and helps in time of need.

We may get busy in our lives, and rush from one situation to another, and can feel overwhelmed. Amid our frantic activity, we should stop, calm down, and dwell upon the Lord.

God created the Sabbath day for mankind to rest. Some people have a hard time relaxing or taking vacations. Some people don't see the need to take time in their lives to reflect and think about God. We should never be so busy that we can't stop and consider the goodness of God and how He blesses us.

The poem is talking about being at the beach and collecting seashells, and the verses are talking about the mountains falling into the sea. Think about the contrast.

The verses are also talking about when we are in conflicts; we should stay calm and trust upon God to take care of us. Do you trust in God in times of conflict?

Why will God be exalted among the nations and the world?

In this busy world, it is vital for individuals to take time to be alone and regroup their thoughts and rest. God created the heavens and the earth and "rested" on the seventh day. What are some of the benefits of resting?

Taking family vacations can be a way of creating memories that will last a lifetime, like taking seashells home from the beach. What are some of your pleasant memories of vacations?

How can you "be still and know that I am God?"

51. LAZARUS AND THE RICH MAN

I am just Lazarus
For food, I have to beg,
I've only got one coat
And sores upon my leg.

I see the rich man
Pass me by each day,
When I ask for alms
He turns and looks away.

And when I had died
In the grave, I was laid,
The rich man also died
Respects to him were paid.

But now I'm in Paradise
No longer am I poor,
For I had believed in Christ
When He knocked upon my door.

And I see the rich man
Over across the fire,
For he never trusted Christ
To be his only savior.

"But Abraham replied, 'Son, remember that in your lifetime you received your good things, while Lazarus received bad things, but now he is comforted here and you are in agony. And besides all this between us and you a great chasm has been set in place, so that those who want to go from here to you cannot, nor can anyone cross over from there to us.'" (Luke 16: 25,26)

~ ~ ~ ~ ~

The Bible speaks of hell as a real place, just as heaven is a real place. Lazarus didn't go to heaven because he was poor and the rich man didn't go to hell because he was rich, because it is not what we have on earth that determines where we spend eternity. It is our faith in Christ that saves us.

The Bible states that we are all sinners and cannot go to heaven with sin on us. Jesus, who is God, became sin for us and died on the cross in our place. Christ died for everyone, but it is up to us to trust in His payment. Christ died for the rich and the poor. No one has to go to hell, because God wants all to be saved and trust Jesus as their savior. Jesus died for all.

The Bible says that when people died before Christ's death on the cross, they were saved by faith, by looking forward to Jesus's death and resurrection. Christ hadn't died on the cross yet, so all Christians went to a place called Paradise, or also called Abraham's bosom. What does the verse above say was between the unsaved and saved in Christ's time?

After Christ's death on the cross, Christians went to heaven. Where do you think Lazarus is now?

Why did Lazarus go to heaven?

Some people, including some Christians, do not believe that there is a hell. Why or why not?

What is your belief in life after death?

The rich man wanted Abraham to send Lazarus to his brothers to warn them about where he was. If you do believe that hell as a real place, should you be telling others about accepting Christ as their savior so they can go to heaven?

52. THE NIGHT SNOW

Snow is falling softly down,
   Making nature pure white,
Over in the distant town
   There comes a glowing light.

Through the darkness comes around,
   The moon shines forth its light,
The beauties of God still abound
   In the quietness of the night.

"He spreads out the northern skies over empty space, He suspends the earth over nothing. He wraps up the waters in His clouds, yet the clouds do not burst under their weight. He covers the face of the full moon, spreading His clouds over it. He marks out the horizon on the face of the waters for a boundary between light and darkness." (Job 26:7-10)

~ ~ ~ ~ ~

God created the heavens and the earth in six days, according to Genesis. It is important for Christians to believe that God created the heavens and the earth because the Bible says He did. If we do not believe what the Bible says about creation, then how can we trust that the rest of the Bible is true?

God created nature for us to enjoy. He created vast mountains, valleys, and rivers. In the thunderstorms, His power can be heard, and in the soft snow, His gentleness can be seen.

After a busy day, we can relax and dwell upon what God has done for us. We can sit and watch the snow gently falling and know that God is taking care of us.

What is your view on God creating the heavens and the earth?

Why is it important to believe in creation?

If you are interested in learning more about creation, there is a variety of books and literature that you can read on the subject.

God created the heavens and the earth for our enjoyment. Have you ever been outside in nature and dwelled upon what He has created?

Have you ever sat quietly at night and watched the snow softly falling?

Sometimes people get too busy in their lives to sit back and enjoy the beauty of nature. Will you take the time this week to go outside and observe the awesomeness of what God has made for us to enjoy?

53. A DREAM IS LIKE A STAR

A dream is like a star
That guides our thoughts at night
They give our life much meaning
Makes the future seem more bright.

But there can be a time
That the star will burn away
Our lives will seem pointless
And dark will be our day.

To give our life new meaning
The past behind is far
We need to focus clearly
Upon another star.

"His brothers then came and threw themselves down before him. 'We are your slaves,' they said. But Joseph said to them, 'Don't be afraid. Am I in the place of God." You intended to harm me, but God intended it for good to accomplish what is now being done, the saving of many lives. So then, don't be afraid. I will provide for you and your children.' And he reassured them and spoke kindly to them." (Genesis 50:18-20)

~ ~ ~ ~ ~

Joseph's brothers were jealous of him and wanted to kill him, but instead, they sold him to a caravan that ended up in Egypt. While there, Joseph was unjustly accused by Potiphar's wife and spent a few years in prison. Pharaoh took Joseph out of prison and made him the second ruler in all of Egypt.

Joseph didn't let his circumstances keep him down. Throughout everything that happened to him, he trusted God and was blessed by Him.

When negative things happen to us, do we stay stuck and feel like life is over? God wants us to trust in Him, and to see what new doors He will open. We should set new goals and enjoy the life God has given us.

Have you ever been jealous of someone? How did you handle your jealousy?

Joseph's brothers were jealous of him. How did they handle their feelings?

What did Joseph say to his brothers about the sins that they committed against him?

Sometimes people become disappointed in life because things didn't turn out the way they thought they would. Living in regret doesn't help us in our present life. Are there any regrets in your life that you haven't come to terms about?

Letting go of negative things and regrets in the past is emotionally healthy. Why is that statement correct?

What is your star in life? Write below what you are focused on accomplishing.

54. YOUR WILL LORD

All blessings that
   You give,
Within my soul
   To live.

Your will Lord,
   I seek,
Within my heart
   To keep.

Love You've shown
   My way,
Keeps me through
   Each day.

Your will Lord
   Not mine,
Is etched across
   The time.

"When Jesus reached the spot, He looked up and said to him, 'Zacchaeus, come down immediately. I must stay at your house today.' So he came down at once and welcomed Him gladly. All the people saw this and began to mutter, 'He has gone to the guest of a sinner.' But Zacchaeus stood up and said to the Lord, 'Look, Lord! Here and now I give half of my possessions to the poor, and if I have cheated anybody out of anything, I will pay back four times the amount.' Jesus said to him, 'Today salvation has come to this house, because this man, too, is a son of Abraham. For the Son of Man came to seek and to save the lost.'" (Luke 19:5-10)

~ ~ ~ ~ ~

Zacchaeus was a tax collector and a short man who wanted to see Jesus. He climbed a tree as Jesus passed by, and Jesus called out to him. Zacchaeus was seeking out Jesus and wanted to get to know Him.

Jesus is calling out to everyone to come to Him and receive eternal life. God also has a plan for each of us. Just as He changed Zacchaeus's heart, God can change our hearts. Are you willing to seek God and have His will in your life?

Why did Zacchaeus climb the tree?

The people complained when Jesus went to Zacchaeus's home. Why do you think they got upset?

For whom did Jesus come to Earth?

We are saved by faith in Jesus, not by works. After we are saved, God wants us to serve Him. What did Zacchaeus do after he trusted Christ as his Savior?

Zacchaeus's life was changed when he met Jesus. How has your life changed since you became a Christian?

Christ came to seek and save the lost. Everyone can trust Christ as their Savior, and God wants all to be saved. Have you trusted Jesus as your Savior? If so, do you want to live for Him?

Please check out my other books available on Amazon.

- JOY In Overcoming Depression Through God's Word
- JOY In Knowing Jesus Through God's Word

My next book will be released Dec. 2019.

- Poetry and Devotions for the Soul for Kids

Thanks for reading. I hope you enjoyed my book. If you found it helpful, would you please leave a review on Amazon.

ABOUT THE AUTHOR

Sandy Bohon is a Licensed Mental Health Counselor practicing in central Florida. She received her bachelor's degree from Florida Bible College and a Master of Counseling degree from Liberty University. Through her counseling experience and Biblical knowledge, her writings can help you achieve the joy back in your life through putting your focus on Jesus and his Word.

In her spare time, Sandy enjoys spending time with her family, going to the beach and gardening. She has 3 adult children, 3 grandchildren and a rescue puppy, Bailey.

Made in the USA
Monee, IL
15 January 2022